Healthy Animal's Journal

What You Can Do to Have Your Dog or Cat Live A Long and Healthy Life

Christina Chambreau, DVM

To your animals glowing health!

with
Catalina Smith
and
C. Liane Luini

R. Catalina Smith

5·2010

www.searchholistic.com

TRO Productions
Sparks, Maryland

Published by
TRO Productions
908 Cold Bottom Road
Sparks, MD 21152

ISBN 1-88660-05-0

This book is dedicated to Beasley,
a very special cat who led me to
new paths of healing.

A loving thank you to my husband and daughter,
Mort and Tracie Orman, who support me in lecturing
around the country, where I continue to learn loving and
healing approaches from my teachers, colleagues
and incredibly caring animal guardians.
A deep thank you to all the animals in my life
and practice—it is your journey of healing that inspires
every one of us to have hope for health, caring and generosity.

I would especially like to thank each person who has asked
for this book, who has pushed me to complete it or
who has shared with me their wonderful ideas,
comments and love for their animals.

Your Animal Companion Can Be Super Healthy And Live A Longer, Happier Life

YOU Are The One Who Knows What Is Best For Your Animal

HEALTH QUESTIONNAIRE

1. Is your companion animal acting old, getting stiff, or having trouble jumping?

2. Has there been treatment by a veterinarian for any problem more than one time per year?

3. Are there problem behaviors?

4. Does your dog smell "doggy" and need bathing every few months or more?

5. Does your dog or cat have mouth odor or tartar on the teeth?

6. Have you noticed that anyone in the family is becoming allergic to your animal?

7. As the years pass, is your companion showing less interest and happiness in life?

8. Would you like a keepsake of your animal's accomplishments and specialness?

If you answer yes to any of the following questions, keeping a journal would strongly benefit your animal companion.

Keeping This Journal Is The First Most Important Step

Healthy Animal's Journal
Table of Contents

SECTION THREE: DIFFERENT APPROACHES TO HEALTH

SECTION FOUR: BLANK PAGES WAITING FOR YOU TO FILL

Your Animal's Biography Page

Your Animal's Timeline of Health and Major Events

Your Animal's Journal Pages

Your Animal's Treatment Summary Page (last page in the book)

HOW THIS BOOK WILL HELP
YOUR ANIMAL BE HEALTHIER

1. You know your companion animal is **currently ill** or on any medication, conventional or holistic, and you want to know if the treatment is truly healing or just causing temporary improvement.

   This journal will allow you to:

   a. Track all symptoms: ill ones as well as happy traits. You can evaluate the progress of the whole animal as well as specific symptoms.

   b. Evaluate your animal's response to any treatment or lifestyle change. You will begin new treatments, find different practitioners or change diets and lifestyles as needed. An animal can become more ill even as his more superficial symptoms get better (shot stops the itching, but dog develops Cushing's disease). He can have a temporary worsening of superficial symptoms in the process of healing (itching is worse for a few weeks, but the separation anxiety ceases).

   c. Recognize the clues that indicate true health.You set the bar for your companion animal's health goals to a higher level. You will continue treatment until even the early warning signs of ill health have resolved.

2. You think your companion animal is **currently healthy,** so why keep a journal?

   a. A longer life is possible as you tailor diet, treatment and habits to her specific needs.

   b. You will be more careful about choices you make for toys, treats, foods, exercise and lifestyles.

   c. Your companion will be healthier when you start treatment sooner because you understand the energetic basis for health and are carefully observing the whole animal and all her responses.

   d. You will love having a record of all the special occasions, events, mannerisms, antics, awards, accolades, sweet interactions—a book full of love.

WILL THIS TAKE A LOT OF MY TIME?

This journal has been designed to make record keeping easy and practical since I would rather you have time to play with your animals, help the environment, rescue animals or otherwise make a difference in the world. I know you would do anything to benefit your companion animal's health. Once you are in the habit of using the journal it will take no more than a few minutes a day.

HOW OFTEN DO I MAKE ENTRIES?

Like most good habits, daily activity is best. Aim to write in your *Healthy Animal's Journal* every day. Since this is a memory book, you will have more wonderful memories if you make entries every day. This way you will not miss an early warning sign of ill health.

OVERVIEW OF THIS HEALTH GUIDE AND JOURNAL

Optimum Health

In this first section you will learn how healthy your animal can be. Your goal is to know how to evaluate your animal's health by recording the subtle signs of ill health as well as obvious illnesses. Learn how healthy and how long he can live. Discover if your animal is becoming more or less healthy with every treatment. Your goal is to have her become healthier over time.

Using the Journal

Next you will learn how to use this journal, why it is important to keep track of fun and healthy activities as well as ill symptoms. Once you learn about keeping this journal, you have a choice. You can skip directly to the blank pages and begin recording symptoms and memories. Or you may first want to read about different treatment approaches that can further improve health.

Different Approaches to Health

What if you discover that your animal is less than healthy? What if you are already seeking a different treatment approach? The third section is full of information about the many different healing options that are available. Because you are keeping the journal and tracking the symptoms, you can try a new diet, try massage or other new treatment and be able to tell how much it helps your animal. Areas covered are nutrition, vaccination and different ways of treating problems and preventing illness (acupuncture, herbs, flower essences homeopathy and more). You will learn ways to find veterinarians and other healers for your animal's health team, how best to work with them and ways you can directly heal your animal.

Your Animal's Journal Pages

Finally, the journal pages await your pen. The tips and quotes and cartoons will entertain you as you fill the pages with cherished memories and clues as to the health status of your companion animal.

Welcome to the journey of having each of your animals attain their highest level of health. You are joining an elite group of people who know how to maximize the health of their animals.

SECTION ONE: OPTIMUM HEALTH

HOW HEALTHY CAN YOUR ANIMAL BE?

Caring people like yourself who have attended my "Improve Your Animal's Health" classes always comment that they know when their animals are super healthy. Most people agree that health is a glowing hair coat, bright eyes and high energy. Health is an absence of illness. Healthy animals live longer than most people have come to expect.

During the past 40 years of working with animals as a veterinarian and veterinary technician I have learned some early indicators of ill health. Since shifting to the use of the holistic paradigm I have learned many more. My colleagues and I realize that most animals can become healthier. When a person is tracking every measurement of health (current and prior problems and overall status) in the veterinary records and/or in an owner-kept journal, changes are noted in minor as well as major problems. Our animals have many symptoms now being considered normal which represent an underlying energy imbalance and warn of impending illness. As we cure animals of "disease," we find that these "normal" things go away, too. What a joy for you to be able to document what helps cure your animals.

Your commitment to your pet's health is strong, so don't be satisfied with your animal's health until there are no more of the symptoms listed in the early warning signs section. Start treating young animals as soon as you see some of these clues. Keeping a lifetime journal will give you a tool to maximize the health of your animals as you will see trends of decreasing or improving health and can take steps to correct the problem. You can evaluate how your animal is responding in all ways to the treatment by your veterinary and healing team, as well as to diet and environmental changes. By recording the wonderful and touching activities of your beloved companion, you will also have a joyous lifetime memory book.

Now, read the following early warning signs and notice any that are currently present in your animal.

EARLY WARNING SIGNS OF ILLNESS IN DOGS AND CATS

BEHAVIOR: Fear of loud noises, thunder, wind; dog barks too much and too long; suspicious nature; timidity; licking things and/or people; irritability; indolence; eating dog stool or cat stool (it seems to be normal for dogs to eat horse, cow and rabbit manure); feet sensitive to handling; aggressiveness at play; destructiveness; biting when petted too long (cats, especially on rump); hysteria when restrained; irritability; not covering stool and not using litter box (cats); clumsy; slow to learn; too clingy or not affectionate.

DIGESTIVE SYSTEM: Mucus on stools, even occasional; tendency to diarrhea with least change of diet; constipation or hard stools; obesity or thinness; bad breath; poor appetite; excessive appetite; finicky appetite; sensitivity to milk, meat, or any specific food; craving weird things, especially non-food items like paper and plastic; constipation; hard, dry stools; loss of teeth; bad breath; pale gums; red gums; (a red line where the teeth go into the gum, above one or more teeth); vomiting often; tartar accumulation. Stiffness when getting up, early hip dysplasia. For cats only: thirst—a super healthy cat on good food will drink at most once a week and many will never drink since they absorb enough from their diet unless on dry food; vomiting hairballs (or the hairball gagging type of vomit even if hairballs do not come up) more than 1-2x/year; loss in the bounce in their step; inability to jump up to their favorite places.

SKIN: Doggy smell or odd odor in any species; attracts fleas a lot; dry coat, oily coat, dry, dull lackluster coat; excessive shedding; chronic ear problems—waxy discharge, frequent recurrence of mites; eye discharge, tearing, or matter in corner of eyes; "freckles" on the face (cats); loss of whiskers (cats); attracts fleas a lot; not grooming well; fragile claws.

TEMPERATURE: Sensitive to heat or cold; low grade fevers. Healthy normal body temperature for cats and dogs is 100-101.5.

A HEALTHY CAT will have a shiny coat, use the litter box normally, eat a wide variety of foods (almost any fresh food and many processed foods), be perky and active, be able to jump to normal heights, and impress people with the "glow" of health.

A HEALTHY DOG will be well behaved, smell nice, eat a wide variety of foods, love a wide range of temperatures and types of exercise, be agile and happy.

EARLY WARNING SIGNS OF ILL HEALTH
IN OTHER SPECIES

How would they be in the wild? Is this really health? Learn what is normal by observing, networking on the Internet, speaking with veterinarians and naturalists. Be open for more health.

Rabbits—red line, black teeth, eating roots.

Goats—stiffness, joint swelling, teeth problems.

Cows—poor milk production, poor digestion.

HOW LONG CAN ANIMALS LIVE?

Over the years that I have been in practice, I have seen a sharp decline in the life spans of many animals. When people begin tracking symptoms and experimenting with different approaches to nutrition and treatment, many of the animals live a longer life.

- In a lecture to 50 Rotweiller breeders, most said their dogs were dying at 6-8 years of age, many of cancer. Three said they customized their approaches by observing what was best for each dog and their dogs lived to 14 and did not get cancer. These three had changed their nutritional approach and were following the updated immunology recommendations for fewer vaccines.

- In a recent study, over two hundred German Shepherds in several kennels are having litters and performing in shows at 10 years of age, and living to 16. Most Shepherd owners are thrilled when their dogs live past 10 years of age.

- One client remembers her childhood Golden Retriever living to 21 (she was 8 when he died) and Dr. Marty Goldstein's own holistically treated Golden lived to 19.

- Great Danes can live to 10-12 years old (current average is 3-6), cats 18-25 (10-12 is now accepted by many practitioners as normal), horses 35 (20 is now the average), Scottish Deerhounds 14-16 (10-12 is normal, now), Irish Wolfhounds 10-13 (5-6 is quoted in the literature).

While this book is about keeping your dogs and cats healthier, all the principles of tracking symptoms in a journal apply to horses, goats, cows, rabbits, hamsters, birds—every species, even people.

STEPS TO SUPER HEALTH

The path to health can be a roundabout journey; just as it can be for humans, or health may be achieved with one simple intervention. Every animal has different needs. Just as there are some basic guidelines for healthy people, the following are health guides for your animals.

Educate yourself

We live in the information era with access to advice from many different sources—your current veterinarian, specialist veterinarians, and holistic veterinarians using acupuncture, homeopathy and other non-conventional approaches. Web sites and Internet news groups abound for veterinary colleges, breed organizations, specific medical problems, different approaches to nutrition, supplements, vaccines, parasite prevention, behavior and more.

There is no "correct" way to become healthy—for people or animals. While many professionals will say that you "must" do this or that, you live with your animal and can best observe what treatment approach is the most healing.

Health Evaluation

Using the tools in this journal and your veterinarian's expertise, evaluate your companion animal's health. Are you perfectly satisfied? Is your companion animal energetic, glowing, bright and alert? Do you think there is the possibility of any improvement?

Select the best veterinarian

Find one or more who will explore new options with you and are willing to work with the different approaches that you are trying. Many people have a local conventional veterinarian, a specialty veterinary practice, one or more holistic veterinarians and several people giving supportive care (grooming, massage, pet sitter, T-Touch, aroma therapist, etc.) Be willing to change or add additional help when needed by your animal.

Provide the best nutrition

Some dogs stop sneezing when switched from one brand of food to another. Some cats become well when started on fresh food while others are not affected by any diet changes. Sometimes improvement does not begin until supplements or different foods are started. By tracking the current symptoms and energy level you will know what nutritional approaches are best.

Choose your vaccine protocol

Your decision will be based on any problems your animal has had when vaccinated and the animal's current health status as well as local risks of a specific disease. It may depend on what you learn from the large amount of information available from the veterinary colleges, veterinary associations, immunologists, researchers and multiple sources on the web or in the many books (veterinary and lay) written since 1990. Your animal's state of health and risk of illness are factors in the vaccination decisions you make.

Focus on the whole animal

Treat the entire animal, not just current symptoms. Have a perspective on health that attempts to treat the underlying energy level rather than merely the current symptoms. Set a goal of glowing wonderful health and do not settle for a lower level of health. Do not settle for "just getting old", or "all dogs have that problem." Since every animal is different, each may need different types of treatment. There are thousands of animals who benefit from conventional treatment. There are thousands who benefit from acupuncture, or homeopathy, or chiropractic, or flower essences or other modalities.

Discover what makes your animal thrive

Provide the best environment and life style for your individual animal. Some animals need a lot of attention and exercise, some become ill from too much. Your journal will help you observe what is best.

Learn healing techniques

You can learn techniques to help your animal feel better. They range from learning how to best groom and train your animal to healing techniques such as flower essences, Reiki, T-Touch and many more that we will discuss later in this book.

Evaluate response to treatment

This is critically important. Sometimes a current problem disappears yet your animal feels less happy or energetic. For example, itching may continue and yet your animal becomes so energetic and happy that you know you must be doing something right. Keeping this journal is your primary tool to evaluate which therapy is the best for your animal at this time.

WHAT ARE THE DIFFERENT WAYS YOUR ANIMAL RESPONDS TO TREATMENT?

There are many possible treatments for any problem, however there are only a few responses to any treatment. Usually we pay attention to the  current problem which either improves, worsens, does not change or goes away completely. To maximize health, it is important to look at the whole animal, including previous problems and energy level, along with the <u>current</u> problems. You can now see why keeping a journal is so important.

The desired cure is when all the symptoms disappear, never to return, and the animal is glowing with health. Healthy animals can, and should, get sick occasionally with acute illnesses that resolve quickly with minimal treatment. The most important clues that you are progressing towards a cure are that your animal is happier and more expressive, and you sense that there is more resilience, more health and centered activity. Some symptoms may continue and resolve slowly. There will often be a brief return of old symptoms or a short worsening of the current symptoms. There could be discharges or even a brief time of skin problems, diarrhea or vomiting while the animal still feels pretty good. A cure occurs when the treatment we have selected stimulates the body to heal itself. The animal first heals on an energetic level. The body, especially on a cellular level, resolves both current ailments and the tendency to become ill. Improvement will be quick if the animal has been sick a short time, and should take longer if the illness is longstanding.

If your cat has been itching for 5 years, it may take 5 - 10 months to completely resolve the itching. If the itching goes away more quickly, palliation or suppression have probably occurred and that is not good in the long run. When there is severe diarrhea for one day, you could expect it to disappear in a few hours. If you find you must re-treat frequently to keep the symptoms in check, or your animal feels worse overall even though the main problem is still gone, you need to talk with your practitioner or consult with someone new.

With a cure, the symptoms slowly go away, and the animal feels better in every way. For example:

- After years of taking aspirin for his painful joints, **Beau** received acupuncture treatments for about 6 months. As long as he returns for a follow up treatment when stiffness begins (no more than 3 times a year), he can leap up the steps, has a great appetite, glowing hair coat and is much more clever and engaging than before.

- **Baby** had been receiving steroid injections for 8 years at an ever-increasing frequency, finally every 6 weeks, to keep her from licking her abdomen raw and bloody (diagnosed as Feline Endocrine Alopecia). She had not become more ill in any other way. This is an example of palliation. After nine months of homeopathic treatment her abdomen was free of lesions. She lived 10 more years and never had skin lesions again. One year later, she recovered quickly from an upper respiratory infection for which 2 other cats in the house had to be treated for 2 weeks. A year after that she again recovered quickly with no treatment from the same fever of unknown origin that the fourth and fifth cat in the house suffered with for a week or so. She was active and healthy until close to the end of her life. That is a cure.

Palliative treatment results in a quick resolution of symptoms, but they keep coming back, need to be retreated frequently and there is no overall improvement in energy level, attitude or resolution of minor problems.

- The poodle **Jacques** got diarrhea after eating garbage and was given antibiotics and antispasmodics. He felt better by the next day. However, it seemed as if his stomach was sensitive for he would 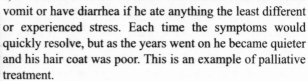 vomit or have diarrhea if he ate anything the least different or experienced stress. Each time the symptoms would quickly resolve, but as the years went on he became quieter and his hair coat was poor. This is an example of palliative treatment.

- **Hershey**, a chocolate lab, became slightly stiff and lame when he was 3 years old. The owner started supplementing with a glucosamine supplement and the limping ceased. If they stopped the supplement, he became lame again. When he was 6 years old his limp had slowly returned, they doubled the glucosamine and the limp went away. When he was 8 years old he developed an incurable degeneration of the spinal cord, common in older dogs. This is an example of palliation. Something (the glucosamine) alleviates the symptom, but does not heal the underlying imbalance causing the problem. Had these owners been keeping a journal, monitoring other symptoms and treating the underlying energy problem, he might not have developed degenerative myelopathy.

Suppressive treatment causes the current symptoms to quickly go away but more severe symptoms appear, and the animal feels no better or may even have less energy. For example:

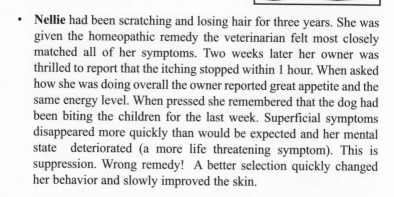

- **Fluffy** received a steroid injection for the ulcers in her mouth that appeared after vaccinations. Within days the ulcers disappeared, yet she became lame on the left front foot, drooled copiously, drank a lot and slept most of the time.

- **Nellie** had been scratching and losing hair for three years. She was given the homeopathic remedy the veterinarian felt most closely matched all of her symptoms. Two weeks later her owner was thrilled to report that the itching stopped within 1 hour. When asked how she was doing overall the owner reported great appetite and the same energy level. When pressed she remembered that the dog had been biting the children for the last week. Superficial symptoms disappeared more quickly than would be expected and her mental state deteriorated (a more life threatening symptom). This is suppression. Wrong remedy! A better selection quickly changed her behavior and slowly improved the skin.

If you think your practitioner is not curing your animal, express your concerns. Request a referral or simply choose another veterinarian.

SECTION TWO: USING THIS JOURNAL

KEEPING THE JOURNAL

THE FIVE KEY PARTS OF YOUR ANIMAL'S JOURNAL

I. Biography page covers all the general information about the history of your animal before coming to you.

II. Bookmark (inside back cover)
   a. Master symptom list.
   b. Physical exam outline with early warning signs of disease.

III. Timeline of health.

IV. Blank journal pages for you to fill.

V. Treatment summary pages.

FIVE EASY STEPS TO START THE JOURNAL

1. **Fill out the biography page and insert the corners of a favorite photo into the slits on the front cover.** Where did you get the animal and when? Any history you can glean. What kind of situation did she come from? How did he react when first with you? Where did he sleep? What temperature did she prefer? Write any memories of the first few days in your home. Include any drawings or pictures from that time. (Now is a great time to record in your other animals' journals how they reacted to this new family member.)

Let's see what Tippy's family writes in his biography.

Tippy's Biography

We bought Tippy when he was 16 weeks old from a young couple who didn't have enough time to spend with him. He urinated in the house a lot when left alone. Got all his vaccinations and had diarrhea since. He's a black cocker mix with white tips to his ears and tail. He was so happy to see us, but so weak that he seemed to tip over on his side, so we named him Tippy.

2. **Tear off the Master Symptom List/Physical Exam Guide from the book cover. Once it is filled out, use it as a bookmark.**

Fill out the Master Symption List

Having easy access to all previous symptoms will make it easy to keep the daily record. This heavy sheet is numbered and the first five lines are filled in with qualities you need to evaluate each day: overall energy level/alertness, emotional state/social interaction, appetite, thirst and vaccinations. Now check your old records and the memory of everyone in your home to compile a complete list of all previous symptoms. Record every prior problem followed by the date it occurred. Do not repeat a symptom if it recurs. Write the dates of recurrences beside the original date. Record the date of all vaccines by number 5. Use initials to indicate the different vaccines given: DHLPP (the five in one vaccine usually given annually), D (Distemper only), P (Parvo only), Ly (Lyme), B (Bordetella—kennel cough), R (Rabies), O (other). Be as brief as possible. The blank journal sheets are the place to describe everything about each vaccination episode.

What does Tippy's family say about starting the Master Symptom List?

Tippy's Master Symptom List
1. Overall energy/alertness
2. Emotional state/social interactions
3. Appetite
4. Thirst
5. Vaccines DHLPP, B, Ly, at 7 wks, 12, 14, & 16wks, R 16 wks, 4/97, 6/98, R 16 wks, 5/97, 3/2000
6. Diarr 8wks - 6/96, 5/2000
7. Worms 9/97
8. Hairloss 1/98
9. Obesity 4/98
10. Hypothyroidism 6/98
11.
12.
13.
14.
15.
16.
17.

We started Tippy's journal when he was 4 years old. We had kept notes before and thought this journal would be easier to use, and help improve his health and provide nice memories for future reference.

We recorded diarrhea for symptom 6, because he had diarrhea for the first 5 months of life, then had it at 4 years of age. Note the two dates beside "diarrhea". We recorded "worms" for number 7 because he had tapeworms one time. We remembered that he used to be afraid of thunderstorms and recorded that as number 6 and wrote that Rescue Remedy stopped the fearfulness. The cause of symptom 8 (hair loss), 9 (obesity) and 1 (lethargy) was determined by the veterinarian to be hypothyroidism, which is now number 10.

Do a Physical Exam

Read through the Physical Exam and Early Warning Signs of Disease side of the bookmark which is an outline of how to briefly examine your animal, looking for those clues that indicate your animal needs some changes in lifestyle or treatments to be fully healthy. Now that you are up to date on the Master Symptom List, follow the instructions to determine if there are any early indicators of ill health present now or that you can remember from the past to add to the Master Symptom List. Record each of these on the master list and describe them in detail in the journal as you did with all the other symptoms. Next time you are with your veterinarian, ask her to show you what she looks for when doing a physical examination and make notes about this on the Physical Exam card.

How To Do The Physical Exam And Note Early Warning Signs Of Ill Health

Eyes: Look for a change in color in the colored part of the eye (iris). Are the white parts red and irritated? Does the center of the eye (pupil) seem dark black, or white? Is the pupil wide open or tiny? If you shine a light in the eye or point the head toward the light does the pupil get smaller? Any discharge? If so what color? Any smells? Lids—Any bumps or warts, hair loss? Test vision by quickly pushing your fingers towards the eye as if you were going to poke out the eye. Your animal should blink in protection. Sometimes they trust you so much they won't blink, so do not worry too much about non-blinking—just record it in the journal.

Nose: What is the color and is there any change (especially a loss of color)? Any discharges? Sneezing? Itchiness (Rub the nose and see if your animal really wants a lot more rubbing). Scabs? Flaking?

Face: Have any whiskers fallen out? Is there hair loss anywhere? Excessive salivation? Any crusting around the mouth, especially in the corner? Any "rodent ulcers" or spots on the lips? Any discoloration like freckles on the lips, or skin or nose?

Mouth: Describe the color of the gums. Look for a red line where the teeth go into the gums. Check all the upper teeth/gum margins for this. It may be over one tooth or many. Any teeth loss, tartar, broken off tips? Look at the tongue. Some animals will not let you look. Wait till they yawn, then add this part of the physical. Describe the odor of the mouth.

Ears: Color, odor, discharge, hair loss. Describe both the ear and any discharges.

Neck: Feel both sides and under the jaw to feel for lymph nodes (firm swellings that should be there, but not too big). Any other lumps or skin problems.

Front legs: Starting with the shoulders. Feel both sides at the same time to notice any differences. There are lymph nodes in the armpit. How are the elbows? The feet?

Nails: Cracked, thickened, shredding, sensitive to touch, need trimming?

Chest: Try to listen to the heart and notice the frequency of the breaths and the heart beat, if you can.

Abdomen (Belly): Push and prod a little. Do you feel any odd lumps inside? They may be normal, but jot them down till next exam. Nipples look ok? Any discharge from the penis? Can you feel the bladder? Do you see any fleas?

Rear legs: Again, feel both at the same time, starting with the hips. Watch your animal walk and note anything that seems different or abnormal to you. There are lymph nodes behind the knees. Pain, heat, swelling are all to be noticed. Examine the rear feet as you did the front ones.

Skin: Any lumps or bumps? Measure them and record where they are located.

Hair: Greasy. dry, brittle, odor. Brush your hand over the coat firmly. Does a lot of hair shed out?

Temperature: Occasionally take a rectal temperature. A healthy dog or cat will have a body temperature of 100-101.5.

The following is a sample summary of what you have noticed over the last month.

Attitude: More or less playful, happy, aggressive, fearful, active.

Generals: Change in preference for heat and cold, thirst, appetite, stool or urine. Does the body feel cold or hot to your touch?

Tippy's family did the physical and found:

As we examined Tippy we saw a red line on the gum over the left tooth and brown wax in the ears. We added these to the Master Symptom List with today's date.

Tippy's Master Symptom List
1. Overall energy/alertness
2. Emotional state/social interactions
3. Appetite
4. Thirst
5. Vaccines *DHLPP, B, Ly, at 7 wks, 12, 14, & 16wks, R 16 wks, 4/97, 6/98, R 16 wks, 5/97, 3/2000*
6. *Diarr 8wks - 6/96, 5/2000*
7. *Worms 9/97*
8. *Hairloss 1/98*
9. *Obesity 4/98*
10. *Hypothyroidism 6/98*
11. *Red gum line 5/10/2000*
12. *Ear wax 5/10/2000*
13.
14.
15.
16.
17.

3. **Construct a Timeline of Health** from your earliest memories of this animal until the present. Add to the timeline anytime a new symptom, major life event or treatment occurs. Remember to use a different color for the positive live events. Tippy's timeline would include all vaccines, diarrhea, ribbon in obedience class, ticks, move to VA, fleas, fear of storms, tapeworms, new cat, finished agility course, owner sprained ankle, few walks, tired, hair loss, hypothyroid. Each time you make a timeline or journal entry, rate your pet's overall energy level. You could use 10 for super energetic and 5 for not very active and 1 or 2 for quite ill and lethargic. You could devise another scale that you write on the page like A – active, B-basically ok, C – couch potato, D-Dull, F-flat out.

Tippy's Timeline of Health and Major Events	
1-4/96 DHLPP, B, Ly(x4), R	4/98 Energy (4) Fat
1-5/96 diarrhea	6/98 DHLPP. Diagnosed as hypothyroid and put on Soloxine. (4) energy.
4/96 Acupuncture	
6/96 no diarrhea and won ribbon in obedience class	4/2000 Rabies - 3 year
1/97 moved to Virginia	5/2000 Diarrhea
4/97 DHLPP	
5/97 R	
6/97 fear storms worse	
9/97 tapeworms	
11/97 got spiffy, a new cat. Fear of storms gone with Rescue Remedy. Finished agility training	
1/98 I sprained my ankle and he lost hair	
2/98 Seemed low energy (5) and wanted shorter walks	

4. Begin to **fill out the blank journal pages**, using a pretty color for positive events. Begin with the first symptom on the Master Symptom List. Write that date and symptom on the first page of the journal. Record every detail you remember about that illness or fun event. Include anything the veterinarian told you, any treatment you remember and how your animal responded to the treatment. Be specific about how things looked, not just the diagnosis. ("Gingivitis," says the veterinarian. "Why do you say that?" you ask. She shows you the red line above four of the teeth, the pus coming out behind one tooth…etc.) It is important to grade and quantify each symptom so you will be able to measure improvement after different treatments or lifestyle changes. Measure any amounts eaten or drunk that seem unusual, or the size of any masses or raw spots or wounds.

Tippy's family fills in details of the past problems they listed on the Master Symptom List.

3/96 1. 7(1-10) 2. He was friendly and interactive, a real sweetie. He was slightly afraid of loud noises - door slamming, book dropping and when we argued. He seemed to have trouble learning in his obedience classes 3.? 4.? 6. The rescue groups and the veterinary records said Tippy had diarrhea off and on since 8 weeks of age. It began three days after the 2nd set of vaccines. Drugs given included Amoxicillin, Flagyl, Centrine and immodium. 4/5/96 1. 6(1-10) 2. same 3.?4? 6. Began acupuncture and Chinese herbs. Still had diarrhea even on the drugs so stopped all of the drugs.

Tippy's first journal entry was dated March 1996, for the diarrhea that was present at 4 months of age when we brought Tippy home. We remembered that his energy level and alertness was 7 on a scale of 0-10 with 10 being super energetic. He was very friendly and interactive, though afraid of loud noises. We did not remember anything for his appetite or thirst, so put "?" for 3 and 4. For number 6 (the diarrhea) we recorded that it was very smelly and watery and that sometimes Tippy went in the house. We were treating with drugs from the veterinarian which stopped the diarrhea for a few days at a time. He hated taking the pills and seemed nauseous for an hour after taking the drug. We added that to the Master Symptom List. The next entry was April, 1996 when we started acupuncture. The energy level was still a 7 and the diarrhea had pieces of food in with the mucous. It smelled like a dead fish now and even Tippy did not seem to like the smell.

For each entry on the Master Symptom List we continued this process. See how the entries were made on the sample sheets.

6/10/96 1. 9(1-10) 2. same - wonderful dog. His fear of thunderstorms was easy to control by giving him Rescue Remedy. 3. normal 4. normal 6. no more diarrhea. He won a ribbon in his obedience class - we were so proud.	9/12/97 1. 7 2. Sweet and loving. We had fewer storms and he seems less afraid, but it was still a problem
4/97 1. 9 2. was energetic and sweet. 3. & 4. normal. 5. DHLPP and the vet said he was fine. Started Heartworm preventative 5/97 Rabies at a vaccine clinic.	11/97 1. 7 2. We remember him continuing to love his family and he even accepted easily the new cat my daughter wanted. He finished his agility training and we are so proud of him! He
6/97 1. 8 2. just as sweet as ever, but in the last 2 weeks his fear of storms and loud noises has become more severe than ever before. Even the Rescue Remedy only helps a little bit. As I write this in 2000, I am realizing it began shortly after his rabies vaccine. 3. fine 4. fine	did seem less active (of course in retrospect we understand it was the hypothyroid problem). 3. Begging for food a bit more. 4. normal
	2/98 1. 5 (1-10) His energy really was slipping, but we thought it was the winter or my sprained ankle. 2. sweet and loving 3. increased appetite - seems hungry a lot. 4. normal 8. He lost a lot of hair. It came
out in handfuls when we brushed him. Even though the winter was warm I wondered if he had a problem.	hypothyroidism which could be causing all of his problems with energy, weight and coat. We started him on Soloxine.
4/98 1. 4 (1-10) I was starting to worry about his energy - is this normal for an adult? - but was too busy to check it out then and he was ok otherwise. 2. sweet 3. Still was very hungry 4. normal 8.He continues to lose more hair. He is not bald, but his undercoat is very thin. The hair seems dry and brittle, as well. We are bathing him every 3 to 4 week for his dog smell. 9. He was looking quite chubby and I cut out all treats	3/5/2000 1. 7 (1-10) 2. still a great dog, though starting to not greet family as often. 3. normal since on the soloxine. We started feeding fresh food the last year and he loves all foods. 4. Normal thirst 5. Rabies vaccination. This time we used Reiki to help prevent secondary problems. 8. No excess shedding anymore but his coat has never been as shiny as before the thyroid problem. 9. His weight is normal if we limit his
6/5/98 - 1. 4 (1-10) 2. sweet 3. hungry. 4. normal 5. DHLPP 8. Very thin hair. 9. Fat10. The veterinarian diagnosed	commercial diet and exercise him a lot. 11. This red line changes a lot, getting bigger when he does not feel as well.

Examples of how animals may react to treatment include a horse who had a painful ulcer in one eye and had to be forcibly restrained to be treated. After the first treatment with Calendula/Hypericum spray, the horse came to the front of the stall and stuck his head over the door to get the treatment sooner. A cat dumped the water bowl when it contained 4 drops of Rescue Remedy with the water, then turned it over again with 3 drops, stalked by with a growl when 2 drops were mixed with the water and drank it eagerly when only 1 drop of Rescue Remedy was added to the water. These responses are important to record. You may notice a correlation that the treatment causing the most improvement will be sought out by the animal. This is not always the case, of course.

Ask yourself and others in the family if they remember what could have caused the diarrhea. This is especially important for current problems. Were emotional things happening in the family, had the animal just been to the groomer, or vaccinated, did you just get another animal, was a new food started, etc.?

Continue the above process for every symptom on your Master Symptom List. Tippy's completed pages are displayed here.

Tippy's Treatment Summary Page
March 1996 - antibiotics & antispasmodics,
April 5, 1996 - Acupuncture with Dr.
June 1996 - Rescue Remedy (Fears)
Sept 1997 - Centrex for tapes
May 1998 - Soloxine .2 mg daily
4/2000 Vetriscience's Acetylator (diarr)

5.   Finally, **record all treatments** ever given (that you can remember) on _____'s **Treatment Summary Page** at the end of the journal. Start with the last page and work forwards. That way you will not run out of pages. Begin again with the first symptom on the Master Symptom List. Record the date of the treatment(s) given for that condition. This is merely a list of treatments, as the journal pages have the details of administration and reactions to the treatments.

MAKING DAILY JOURNAL ENTRIES

You will use the following sections for daily Journal entries.

  II. Bookmark (inside back cover)
    a. Master Symptom List.
    b. Physical exam outline with early warning signs of disease.
  III. Timeline of Health.
  IV. Blank journal pages for you to fill.
  V. Treatment summary pages.

Because the journal is for wonderful memories as well as symptoms, taking a few minutes each day will assure you do not forget that sweet kiss Tippy gave your son. The following will first give you some tips on keeping the journal, then more specific instructions and sample pages. You may have been making entries for months before you read this section and however you have been keeping the journal is perfect. Everyone does it differently. Remember that the purpose of this journal is to help you focus on the wonderful, happy times and improve health by noting your animal's response to treatments and life style changes. If you are having trouble with keeping this journal there are monthly teleclasses when you can talk with Dr. Chambreau and other people who are seeking ways to keep their animal healthy for many long years. (www.healthyanimalsjournal.com)

So let's begin!! Sit down for your daily session of tracking symptoms.

• Open the journal to the bookmarked place.

• Record today's date.

• First think of any exciting, sweet, nice, clever or profound occurrences that your animal did since you last made an entry (hopefully it was only yesterday!) Record those in bright, happy colors.

• Next, report on the first five preprinted symptoms that are of key importance to overall health. Be as detailed as possible and use quantitative measures whenever possible.

• Then think of any problems that are bothering you now with your dog or cat. See if they are already listed on the Master Symptom List. The Master Symptom List will have some symptoms that occurred only once in their life, and many symptoms that recur, and current concerns that may be new or on-going. If this current symptom was already on the list, write today's date on the Master Symptom List at that symptom. Add any new symptoms or momentous occurrences to the Master Symptom List along with today's date.

- Briefly review all symptoms, even very old ones on the now updated Master Symptom List. Enter the corresponding number of any problem that the animal is experiencing now. There is no need to make an entry on this day in the journal unless a symptom is currently causing problems.

- Quantify each of these symptoms as accurately as possible. Evaluating the response of your animal to any treatment (or diet or exercise change) will depend on knowing how bad things are pre-treatment. Count the warts. Measure the tumors or raw, itchy areas. Draw a picture of the changes on the cornea. Count the number of sneezes per day. Rate the amount of itching on a scale of 0 -10. Describe the odor of the skin, or mouth, or discharge. What time does a problem occur?

- Pay very careful attention to symptoms that occur shortly after a treatment is given.

- Enter the treatment(s) given at this time. Be specific: what time was the remedy given, how long did you do acupressure or TTouch, which new vegetable did you try, etc.

- Periodically, perform the brief physical exam and record any new indications of early illness. If your animal is a puppy or kitten, do your own physical exam once a week until 4 or 5 months old, and then shift to monthly exams. At one year, start doing the checks every 6 months. When the animal has been ill, do them weekly, and then taper off as they regain their health. When they become elderly, do them monthly again. Once a year, or more often if needed, have a veterinarian do a physical to see if there is anything you are missing. If doing the physical exam makes you think that that your companion animal is becoming less healthy in any way, check with your current practitioner or a new one if you feel your animal is not being helped as much as possible. Or try a new diet, different exercise or a different type of healing you have learned to do yourself if you feel the condition of your animal is not too severe.

- If you are treating your animal today, turn to the last pages of your pet's Treatment Summary and record the date (and time may be useful) of any treatments. This is a summary, so be brief.

- Each day, remember to put the most emphasis on the energy, happiness, interactions, appetite and overall sense of how she is doing. If the skin is worse but she feels better, continue your current treatments until you feel there is no further progress.

- Periodically, record special events (illnesses, treatments, shows, activities) on the timeline.

4/24/2000 Tippy is such a sweetheart. He jumped into my bed to wake me up this morning with a sweet kiss and almost purred like a cat. 1.7(1-10) Today is the first day we noticed energy increase. 2. Staying by himself only 20% of the time, and still wanting to run away. The oddest thing - he seemed afraid of his reflection in the TV. 3. App normal since one week after starting Acetylator. He is definitely wanting to eat salty things. We thought so, but now he is running into the kitchen when I sprinkle salt on food. How can he know salt from pepper? 4.	Normal thirst 6. Definitely an improvement since Acetylator. 50% of the time there is a liquid or soft end to his stool containing some undigested food particles. 40% of the time the formed stool is dark and covered in mucus. One time, 2 weeks ago it seemed like his stool just fell out as he was walking and he did not realize it. 8. Shedding less - 20% more than normal. 11. The red line on the gums goes up and down from little to wide, being wide about every 3rd day.Treatment: we consulted with Dr. C for homeopathic treatment since a Reiki friend suggested this. She

Tippy's Treatment Summary Page
March 1996 - antibiotics & antispasmodics,
April 5, 1996- Acupuncture with Dr.
June 1996 - Rescue Remedy (Fears)
Sept 1997 - Centrex for tapes
May 1998 - Soloxine .2 mg daily
4/2000 Vetriscience's Acetylator (diarr)
4/24 - Lyssin 200c

Tippy's Master Symptom List
1. Overall energy/alertness
2. Emotional state/social interactions
3. Appetite 4/24 desires salt
4. Thirst
5. Vaccines DHLPP, B, Ly, at 7 wks, 12, 14, & 16wks, R 16 wks, 4/97, 6/98, R 16 wks, 5/97, 3/2000
6. Diarr 8wks - 6/96, 5/2000
7. Worms 9/97
8. Hairloss 1/98
9. Obesity 4/98
10. Hypothyroidism 6/98
11. Red gum ine 5/10/2000
12. Ear wax 5/10/2000
13.
14.
15.
16.
17.

prescribed Lyssin 200c since the problems seemed worse after the rabies vaccine and many of his symptoms occurred in the Lyssin testings.

4/25/2000

I was home for the afternoon and Tippy curled up beside me after we came home from the veterinarian and slept with his front paw on my leg.

1.7(1-10) His eyes seem brighter. 2. By himself only 10% of the time. No fear of his reflection in the TV. 3. Likes salt. 4. Normal thirst 6. BM - no change 8. Normal amount fur when I petted him and his coat seems to glow. 11. Red line

medium width.

4/26 This morning Tippy was so agile chasing his Frisbee.

1.7(1-10) 2. Seems happy. 3. would not eat his chicken till I put some salt on it.

4. Normal thirst 6. BM Firm with soft end. 8. Little more shedding (could see fur fly when I petted. 11. Red line very narrow. 12. ears were itchy this evening.

4/272000 Tippy is so smart. John came home earlier than usual and Tippy knew before the car came into the driveway to wait in the window. 1.7(1-10) His eye seem brighter. 2. He does not seem to be by himself

more than a normal dog. He gets up and follows me some times when I go from room to room. 3.App fine. 4. Normal thirst 6. BM -very dark today. 11. Red line thin.

4/28/2000 With all the problems today, Tippy was very sweet to the cat who chased Tippy's tail. 1. 7(1-10) His eyes are still bright. 2.Super fear of his reflection in the TV and also in the mirror . 3. He seems desperate for salt to day, even standing in front of it. He did not want to eat until I really salted the food. 4. He backed away from the water as if afraid of it and did not drink.

Tippy's Timeline of Health and Major Events
4/98 Energy (4) Fat
6/98 DHLPP. Diagnosed as hypothyroid and put on Soloxine. (4) energy.
4/2000 Rabies - 3 year
5/2000 Diarrhea
5/2000 A star in agility class

Fun, wonderful happenings in your animal's life are critically important to record for several reasons. Many philosophers and thinkers through the ages have written that our minds act upon our most predominant thoughts. "As a woman thinketh, so is she." "Thought is creative." "Changing your thoughts changes your actions." Focusing on the ill symptoms of your animal can influence how your animal will recover. Many doctors have realized that the more positive a person is, the faster they recover from any treatment. Focusing on the wonderful, fun, sweet, attractive activities of your animal will brighten their days as well as yours. While observing and recording the "ill" symptoms are important, focusing on healthy traits and events is even more important. For even more fun, try writing some or all entries as if your animal was writing for herself. "I ate 5 brussel sprouts today and threw them up 2 hours later. Eeeew—I won't try those again!! Or was it the full moon making me sick? "Use your favorite colors to record the positive events. Second, while we each want our animals to live forever, most of them die long before we do. Having a book(s) full of memories will be a treasure long after our animals are part of the great forever.

When this journal is full, put an updated photo in a new journal book, transfer the Master Symptom List to the next bookmark sleeve and keep this one for reference and memories.

Have a wonderful, fun and nurturing time keeping this journal on your precious companion.

Healthy Animal's Journal

What You Can Do to Have Your Dog or Cat Live A Long and Healthy Life

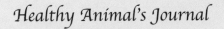

Insert your animal's
photo here

Christina Chambreau, DVM

with
Catalina Smith
and
C. Liane Luini

SECTION THREE: DIFFERENT APPROACHES TO HEALTH

SELECTING THE HEALTHIEST APPROACH

You are the one monitoring your animal's health progress, so you know when something different is needed for great health. Read, talk to other people, talk with your animal health care providers, and take courses. Pay attention to what works and what does not work. Keeping a journal is important so you can look back and see what has gotten better and if problems are getting less frequent and less severe, which is your goal. This journal will help you patiently wait for problems to resolve because you will be able to observe the pattern of the whole animal changing for the better. Patience is definitely an unsung virtue on the road to health. Even if the modality you choose turns out not to be curative, your animal will probably be healthier because you're keeping this journal for him.

Why keeping a journal is a great idea

Knowing what is most healthful for your animal encourages you to keep up with the best and stop whatever does not help as much. Some examples of the usefulness of keeping a journal will help you get started.

- Your son leaves for college and your dog started shaking his head. The ear drops helped the ear, but the dog is acting depressed. Your vet has no more answers but is fine with your suggestion that you try Rescue Remedy (a flower Essence). The ear stays good after one day of itching and the dog stops being depressed. Because you were tracking the overall energy level and emotions you were able to realize that your dog became sad after your son left and could try different things until she was better in all ways.

- Your cat developed diarrhea and you had heard about the holistic approach and found a veterinarian who belonged to the American Holistic Veterinary Medical Association. Though you did all the different things he suggested, you cat's diarrhea was worse and she stopped using the litter box. You went back to your conventional veterinarian who prescribed several drugs that did stop the diarrhea. Your cat then started eating cat litter and plastic bags and when you finished the drugs, the diarrhea returned. When you gave the drugs again the weird appetite continued and she started losing weight and this time the diarrhea was not completely gone. Then you learn Reiki, an energy healing method you do for your own cat, and work with a homeopathic veterinarian. Now your cat is blooming with health and has no diarrhea unless there is a lot of stress. All she needs to stop the diarrhea are a few Reiki treatments from you.

- You may have a wonderful veterinary acupuncturist who thinks you should vaccinate and feed canned food. You follow your heart and feed raw meat and do not vaccinate and continue to use her for acupuncture as long as your animal stays healthy. You may choose processed food and occasional vaccines and wish to work with a homeopathic veterinarian who does not recommend that life style. Stand firm with what you feel is working. Be flexible enough to realize when you (or your practitioner) have made a mistake and it is time for a change. Again, you are responsible for deciding what needs to be tried next for your animal since you are living day to day with your friend. The next step may be conventional drugs, homeopathy, intuitive healing, or one of the hundreds of healing practices accessible today.

You have been keeping the journal. You know your animal is not as healthy as possible and you want to try something different. Five areas have a large impact on our animal's health – nutrition, vaccinations, environment (toxins and social interactions), method of treatment selected and recognizing superficial from deep healing. Start by changing the diet, then look at frequency of vaccines, then explore the many different energy treatment modalities. Some changes can be made yourself and/or choose a holistic veterinarian with whom to work.

NUTRITIONAL APPROACHES

This is really critical—a great diet will help restore health to ill pets and will often prevent health problems in the future. Just as with people, different animals thrive on different types of diets. There are many conflicting opinions about diets for animals just as there are for people.

The following are a few improvements that often happen with a positive diet change:

- Hair is shinier, smoother, odorless, thicker and sheds less
- Mouth is odor free and plaque free
- Ears never need cleaning
- Activity level and social skills are improved

- Stiffness and physical agility improve
- Weight and interest in food become normal
- Some improvement occurs in any current illnesses
- Your pet is happier at meal times

Good—you recognize many of these as early warning signs of illness—improving diet is actually improving overall health.

Many animal guardians and practitioners share the following concerns about diet:

- What are dogs and cats supposed to eat?
- How do I "balance" the diet?
- Will there be improved health and is it safe?
- Do the ingredients need to be from "good" sources?
- How easy is it to prepare or purchase the best diet?
- Will it cost more and where can I find ingredients?

What Are Dogs And Cats Supposed To Eat?

What is the best food for people—the most processed or the least processed? Do some people have to eat mostly fresh food? Yes. Are some people very healthy on more processed food? Yes. The same is true for all animals—the least processed food is the best, yet each animal can be healthy on different foods. As with nutrition for people, very little is really known. Books, experts and conferences on nutrition for people are full of conflicting opinions, but very few people would believe that a single type of canned or dried food would be a super diet. There is a lot of debate about which feeding protocol or brands for animals are the best. There are a huge number of books, web sites and courses available that discuss that author's opinion about the best nutrition for your animal. In this brief overview I will teach you how a carnivore's digestive system works, and some basic diet guidelines that should then make common sense. The way you will discover the best diet for your specific animal is by keeping this journal and evaluating everything, including energy level and happiness as you try different approaches to feeding. In my professional opinion, most animals are less healthy eating processed food than fresh food.

Carnivore Digestive System

Let us look at the carnivore digestive system. What food is it designed for? Dogs and cats have ripping and tearing teeth along with bone crunching teeth (and no grinding teeth); a small muscular stomach and short digestive tract. Most dogs and cats inhale their food rather than chewing. They have digestive systems perfectly designed to process raw muscle and organ meat, bones, skin, fur and the contents of the prey's gut (digested vegetables, nuts and seeds). Cats and dogs do not chew their food to a pulp before swallowing it. Their stomach is designed for receiving big chunks of meat, bones, skin and organs. They absorb little nutrition from grains because they do not chew and have a short digestive system. Because they are adapted to eating a variety of foods many have tolerated processed foods until now.

Canine diet guidelines

Dogs are omnivorous so they can eat vegetables, fruit and maybe even a small amount of carbohydrates along with their animal protein sources. While a few dogs can be healthy on a vegetarian diet, most cannot, so carefully track the chronic disease symptoms to catch any problems early if for ethical reasons you will not feed meat. A fresh meal could be as easy as cutting a whole chicken in half and feeding it for dinner (skin, bones and all), then putting your leftover raw and cooked vegetables into the food processor with a little liquid and some organ meat and feeding that for breakfast. Another meal could be a cooked stew with calcium supplement. Snacks can be anything as long as your dog is healthy. Ill dogs, like people, need the healthiest of ingredients for snacks.

Feline diet guidelines

Cats are obligate carnivores and need mostly meat in their diet. Fruits and vegetables, are best digested when pureed and need only be 5-20% of their diet. Vegetable baby food (preferably organic) is often loved by cats. A meal could be a whole chicken thigh, skin and bone included. Another meal could be liver, vegetables and eggshells pureed in the blender. Another could be hearts (very high in taurine) or other internal organs, with added calcium. Other cats are healthy on freshly cooked fish or meat with added calcium and pureed vegetables. Cats originated in the desert and have "camel" kidneys that are designed to need very little moisture. The moisture needed is completely met by eating raw, cooked or canned food. A normal, healthy cat is not thirsty!!! (You may see them drink rarely.) When cats are fed dry food (most are grain based), they need to drink a lot of water, which overworks their kidneys. Try your best to never feed dry food to cats.

Animal protein sources

Animal protein sources for both dogs and cats include beef, lamb, chicken, turkey, fish, ostrich, buffalo, shellfish, eggs, dairy, venison and any other wild game. All organ meats are great—liver, kidneys, green tripe, lungs, etc. Feeding a variety is important as each protein source has different amino acids, minerals and other nutrients. One sign of health is wide tastes in food, so if your animal is too picky—seek out holistic care.

Balancing your animal's diet

Much debate exists about balancing the diet and the safety of feeding raw bones and meat. You and I do not try to balance each amino acid, vitamin and mineral for each meal. We know that most of us can be healthy if we eat a wide variety of fresh, whole foods. Animals eating "whole prey" and some supplements have a balanced diet with easy and complete absorption of nutrients (with small stools). The processed "balanced" diet is often made of poor quality, high carbohydrate ingredients that are inadequately absorbed (causing large, often smelly stools). Even processed diets made from great ingredients (and there are an ever increasing number of those) do not have the characteristics that the carnivores need—raw, chunks, bone. Some animals thrive on processed grocery brands made with poor ingredients. Many thrive on processed foods (canned and dry) made from great ingredients. The best results, in my experience, are found when feeding mostly a raw meat and pureed vegetable diet for at least part, if not all of the diet. Since you now know that the ideal diet, physiologically, is a raw food diet, and you know that there is no such thing as a "balanced" diet, you are ready to experiment to discover what works best for your unique animal.

Supplements

Calcium supplements are critical if raw bones are not fed. Some veterinarians and guardians are concerned about bones causing injuries and recommend grinding the bones with some meat (a butcher needs to do this). Others say that the digestive system is designed to eat raw meat and bones as in wild dogs and cats. Other than calcium, no expert really knows exactly which animals need which supplements, just as each person may need different supplements. If an animal needs more than a few supplements to stay healthy, more holistic treatment is needed, as healthy animals will get most of their nutrients, vitamins and minerals, from a good diet. However, a "whole food" or "super food" supplement may be helpful since soils often have been depleted of nutrients. Juliette de Bairacli Levy found that animals grazed and selected their own herbal supplements when given access to pesticide free greens, so we know supplements may be needed by all animals. Digestive enzymes and gut flora are useful while the animals are healing, and may even be needed once they are really healthy. Other vitamins and minerals that may be needed when feeding a fresh food diet include taurine (cats), Vitamins A, D, C & E, omega oils and herbs. It is good to try different brands, and even rotate as each supplement is from different food sources. If your animal is doing great you can try not using the supplements and keep evaluating through your journal.

Health benefits and safety when feeding fresh food

My professional experience is that 99% of animals are safe on a raw meat diet and 70% see a significant health improvement. I have seen fewer problems with raw bones than with many chew toys. Some authors and experts on animal health fear parasites and bacteria (toxoplasma, E. coli, Salmonella and others). They recommend first washing the meat in grapefruit seed extract or cooking the meats. There is no lessening of nutrition by doing this—just takes extra time. A must to read on the topic of raw meat is *Pottinger's Cats*. A dentist in the 30s fed raw meat, raw milk and cod liver oil to hundreds of cats for 10 years. If he cooked the meat or the milk, their health severely deteriorated. Dr. Jean Hofve, www.LittleBigCat.com, has material about safety of raw meat and does nutritional and healthy animal counseling. Animals normally have bacteria in the mouth, so feeding raw meat will be no different that you preparing meat for yourself. Use good hygiene. An updated list of the best web sites, books, nutritional coaches and magazine articles on nutrition related issues and tips for ease of feeding can be found at www.HealthyAnimalsJournal.com. *The Whole Dog Journal* has excellent articles about the canine digestive tract and evaluating the different processed foods on the market.

An example of health benefits: A new patient's problems were not too severe, so I started with improvements to the diet. Symptoms were mostly behavioral: Susie was in constant movement, could only sit still for minutes at a time; would circle the room for 20-30 minutes when someone came in the house; was poorly behaved when walked on a leash, drooled on walks and in car when excited; jumped up on counters (she is a golden retriever); swallowed anything - socks, paper and got into the trash for food and other items. She shook her head even when there was nothing apparent in the ears and rubbed and scratched her face a lot. She has a history of ear and urinary tract problems. After 3 weeks on a raw food diet the report was: 90% better on the lead with no pulling at all; calmer at all times; ears are only slightly pink now, the skin lost its redness and is now a normal white; she itches her face 80% less; does not get into trash; still eats stool; still drools; she is 20% better when people come to the house and can sit still for 3 minutes rather than 10 seconds; her stools lost their odor; her hair is glowing and a deeper color (common change on good diet). She is now showing increased frequency of urinating and mucus on the stools so it is time now for more in depth treatment (homeopathy, acupuncture, drugs, etc.).

Quality of Ingredients

The following are a few questions that you may want to ponder. What quality of the ingredients is needed for maximum health of your companion? Do chemical additives and preservatives cause health to deteriorate? Do you want to help both your animal's health and that of the planet by asking that products, especially animal products, be ethically raised? Ask how the meat animals are raised – free range or in tiny pens or cages? What have they been fed? Have the vegetables and meat animals been given hormones, pesticides or drugs that may harm you, your animals and the earth? How much processing is acceptable to you and tolerated by your animal?

Personally, I feed mostly free range, hormone free, antibiotic free, locally raised, pesticide and GMO free meats and vegetables to my family (humans and animals). I choose locally raised over organic since I can visit the farms and know their methods. I am willing to occasionally feed packaged, dehydrated meats of unknown origin from companies I know and respect. Some of my clients feed processed food part of the time and fresh part of the time. Most of my clients avoid any foods, processed or not, that use a lot of chemicals in their processing. There is no lack of strong opinions about each of these issues — on the internet, in books (many now have outdated information) and in conversations. There is no "expert" you can trust to know all the answers because there is no one correct answer. Always think back to how the carnivore is designed by nature and what you would feed your children.

Selection and/or Preparation of Food

How do you know what is in a processed food? Read the label? But do you understand the words on the label? Do you believe the food company president? Do you believe your veterinarian? Do you believe your neighbor? You can learn to read the ingredients as discussed above. Talk with the company itself. Do you intuitively trust the person you are speaking with? Most of the high quality companies are small and the owners or good representatives are eager to educate you about their food. Many of the best pet food companies taste the food themselves. Some are packaged in human food plants. When feeding processed, many supplements are often needed to keep your animal healthy. Even though some foods add supplements after cooking the foods, it is better to use individual supplements at meal time. Once again you are the expert because you know how your animal feels on each diet. Try different food brands and supplements, then keep the journal and evaluate the impact of the new food on the overall health.

Some people are selecting from the many packaged raw meat diets or "fresh" diets processed in different ways, such as fresh delivered, frozen or freeze dried that are now available. Apply the quality criteria you have chosen to these products as well (organic, free range, GMO free, etc). One company's representative recently told me it is impossible to get free range chickens and the same day another said she gets all her meat from farms nearby that she visits on a regular basis to see the chickens running around outside. Ask as many questions as you need of the producers of the fresh food and processed diets as well.

Feeding a fresh food diet, all or part of the time, can be very easy. As with a person starting a new diet, you may want to use books for guidance, but after a time, follow recipes, feed your own combinations, purchase a prepared raw food product, cook mixtures or give raw meat plus your leftovers. Since each individual animal needs different foods and people have different schedules and abilities, you need to find a feeding program that works for your time schedule and results in improved health for your animal. There are now many books on feeding animals, especially dogs and cats. You must find the best diet for each animal and for yourself as "chef". Often people say it is quicker and more satisfying to feed a fresh food diet. I know the few hours a month I spend preparing and freezing my cats' meals are enjoyable because I know it will improve their health.

If you find it is difficult to feed your animals with fresh food ingredients you need some coaching from the experienced fresh feeders. They may not eat every day, nor at every meal. Have a "meal-time"—don't leave food out.

Cost of feeding a better diet

First, your animals will love what you feed. Second, you will be helping the planet with more healthy choices. You will save money on health care in most animals. Finding fresh ingredients will be a wonderful exploration. You can visit local farms to learn how the animals and vegetables are raised and you save on distribution costs. Remember that wild game is hormone and steroid free even if they eat a small amount of pesticide reared crops. Find butchers who will keep the scraps from game, or hunters willing to bring in the organ meat they clean out in the field, or farmers who have more game meat than they can eat. Ask stores when they discount their almost ready to expire meat and produce. Community Supported Agriculture farms (CSAs) provide good, organic, local produce in most states and will usually have information about healthy reared animals if they do not have livestock themselves. While it is initially time consuming to discover good sources, your animal's health is worth it. Ask the farmer for lower cost meats. The costs of raw meat and vegetables for my two cats is around $70 per month. I have not looked for the least expensive organic, free range meats, rather choose to use the most local. Feeding a high quality processed diet would cost $50-80 per month. I remind people that paying extra for high quality like organic or free range is like making a charitable contribution to the health of our planet.

If the better quality ingredients are not available for you and your animals, grocery store meats and vegetables are still fresh and you can see that the chicken leg is not a tumor or necrotic tissue. Look for "happy meat and happy vegetables wherever you buy," says Dr. Pollak.

Good water is important as well. Filtered is probably the best, but there are many choices. Whatever you feel is best for you will usually be best for your animals. The journal entries will show you if your animal needs something different. Remember to buy the best ingredients.

AN EDUCATED APPROACH TO VACCINATION

Are annual vaccines necessary?

While annual physical examinations by your veterinarian are critically important for the health of your animal, there is growing concern about giving annual vaccines. In my opinion, the best approach to vaccination is to build up the health of animals so they are not susceptible to acute infectious diseases (therefore do not need vaccines). The Veterinary College at Colorado State University says on its web site that there is *"lack of scientific evidence to support the current practice of annual vaccination and increasing documentation showing that over-vaccinating has been associated with harmful side effects."* The American Animal Hospital Association (AAHA) agrees, saying on their web site, *"The argument for continuing current historically practiced regimens is based largely on tradition and the perceived paucity of proof supporting extended duration of immunity."*

Do you receive vaccines every year of your life until you die? No. Why not? Why do animals receive them annually? The Colorado State Veterinary College web site says, *"...the annual revaccination recommendation on the vaccine label is just that—a recommendation without the backing of long term duration of immunity studies, and is not a legal requirement."* The AAHA web site agrees, *"...annual vaccination of small animals for many, but not all, infectious agents is probably no longer scientifically justified... such deviations [not giving annual boosters] from recommended adminis- tration are becoming more common and more widely endorsed and, as such, should be considered an acceptable standard of care."* As early as 1992, Kirk's Current Veterinary Therapy, Vol. 11, page 205, says *"A practice that was started many years ago and that lacks scientific validity or verification is annual revaccinations. Almost without exception there is no immunological requirement for annual revaccination...The practice of annual vaccination in our opinion should be considered of questionable efficacy..."*

An increasing number of vaccines have been encouraged over the last 60 years, often, as AAHA says, *"based on limited scientific evidence."* Yearly, or more often, the average dog receives a combination injection of Distemper, Hepatitis, Leptospirosis, Parainfluenza & Parvovirus. Often given are Bordetella (Kennel Cough), Corona vaccine, and Lyme disease vaccine. Cats are given a combination of Panleukopenia (cat distemper, feline enteritis) and three upper respiratory diseases, Calici, Rhino, and Chlamydia. Often they are also given Feline Leukemia, and available are Feline Infectious Peritonitis and now ringworm vaccine. New vaccines are constantly being introduced, often for diseases that do not cause many problems.

Not every veterinarian agrees with the above. AAHA says, *"Many veterinarians are under the misconception that current recommendations were and are scientifically based when, in fact, they may have less basis than the arguments for change."* You will need to read and do your own research to decide on this aspect of routine care. This journal will be a key factor in deciding how often to vaccinate your animal. Review your notes from the time the last vaccine was given. Were there any negative health conse- quences in the days and months following the vaccines? Pay particular attention to behavior changes. The insert in the vaccines says to give only to healthy animals, so the journal will help you know when your animal is most healthy.

Harm from vaccines

When people keep track of their animal's health or the practitioner is tracking changes in every symptom (subtle or obvious), reactions to vaccines are often noted. Obvious vaccine reactions can also occur and most veterinarians give drugs to "pre-treat" for these reactions when they give the yearly boosters. When Gigi received her first booster at 1 1/2 years of age, she sneezed for a few days. The next year she had asthmatic coughing and needed oxygen and drugs to recover. The third year the veterinarian pre-treated her with diphenhydramine and was ready with steroids and epinephrine to treat the reaction to the vaccine.

Veterinarians are now becoming aware of more serious long term problems from vaccines. The Colorado State Veterinary College site says, *"Of particular note in this regard has been the association of autoimmune hemolytic anemia with vaccination in dogs and vaccine-associated sarcomas in cats—both of which are often fatal."* AAHA says, *"There is definite evidence that biologics carry with them risk and benefit."* The American Veterinary Medical Association (AVMA) says, *"...in1991, veterinarians began to notice a higher than expected number of sarcomas occurring on cats' bodies in places where vaccines are commonly injected. Subsequently, an association between vaccine administration and sarcoma development has been established."* In 2003, researchers confirmed fibrosarcoma tumors are occurring at rabies vaccine injection sites in dogs as well as cats.

Jean Dodds in 1990 reported *"Immune-mediated hematologic disease and transient bone marrow failure are increasingly recognized sequela of...vaccination."* Many ferrets developed fatal green diarrhea the year after owners increased the frequency of distemper vaccination because of fear of distemper." An on-going study at Purdue University has demonstrated that *"the serum of all the vaccinated dogs contains significantly elevated concentrations of antibodies directed against proteins."* They go on to say that this could possibly lead to autoimmune diseases. The web sties and list serves have archived many examples of problems with animals that followed vaccinations.

Homeopathic veterinarians have observed over the last 30 years that most animals need remedies known to counteract negative reaction to vaccines. Acupuncture and other holistic veterinarians have seen that animals responding in a curative way to treatment often relapse after vaccines. Guardians have recorded in their journals that certain ailments (lethargy, vaginal infection, ear problems, digestive upsets, eye discharge and almost any problem) appear within the days to months following vaccination.

New recommendations from AAHA, different veterinary colleges and organizations suggest giving fewer vaccines less frequently and evaluating each animal as to their risk factors. Many now recommend drawing blood and checking the titers (blood tests for the antibodies to specific diseases). Adequate titers are often acceptable to anyone requiring vaccination. A key fact, however, is that having an "adequate" titer does not assure protection.

Alternatives to vaccines and lessening possibilities of reactions

The holistic perspective, as you now know, focuses on the health of the whole animal. A healthy animal is unlikely to get sick (or very sick) even if exposed to infectious agents. Ideally we would never vaccinate, would feed the best diet for each animal (probably using fresh meat and vegetables) and treat the early symptoms that indicate the body is out of balance. If they do develop an infectious disease, it can usually be treated successfully with modalities ranging from conventional to acupuncture to homeopathy. Already having a relationship with a veterinarian who feels comfortable treating infectious diseases is important. Vaccinating an animal does not necessarily protect them from the very diseases for which they are vaccinated. This is because the vaccine may be ineffective or there may be systemic immune weaknesses preventing an immune response.

Animals can be safe from most infectious diseases when not vaccinated, and often life spans and overall health improve. I have heard and read many reports from breeders of significantly longer life spans and even a disappearance of "breed" diseases. Horses getting fewer vaccines often no longer colic, do not have as many hoof problems and live longer. Not vaccinating one large beef cattle herd eliminated calf scours. Animals who are being treated by me usually receive only their legally required rabies vaccinations. Other veterinarians recommendations range from annual to only as a youngster. You must make this very personal decision from the research you have done and with acceptance from your animal's health team.

Nosodes are homeopathic remedies made from the tissues of diseased animals. Many people use nosodes instead of vaccinating. There is little historical or philosophical evidence for this approach. I do not recommend trusting nosodes to give future protection, unless they have already been exposed.

Because the rabies vaccination is legally required in many cities, counties and states, your animals need to receive this one vaccine whenever it is due. Time the administration of this, and any other vaccine that you must get (for travel to certain foreign countries) when the animal is as healthy as possible. Many conventional veterinary oncologists and other specialists agree with the holistic community about not vaccinating animal with cancer or autoimmune problems – even for Rabies. Support the immune system before and after any necessary vaccination with extra Vitamin C, super diet, antioxidants, energy treatments like Reiki or T-Touch, homeopathy or Chinese medicine. Be vigilant about recording in this journal during this time so you can know if the vaccines have had a detrimental effect on your animal.

ALTERNATIVE METHODS OF TREATMENT

You have improved the diet and still your animal is not as healthy as you would like. You are ready to find some approaches different from the conventional ones used so far. As in the field of human health, there are many different approaches for healing. Conventional medicine predominates in the Western world and is taught in most of the veterinary and medical schools. More than 50% of people are now seeking holistic treatment options for themselves and now for their animals as well.

Many different approaches to health

For a moment, do not think about specific symptoms or illnesses. Strive to understand the perspectives of various healing approaches. You may feel more attracted to one than another. Follow your intuition and research that one first. Each of your animals may need a different approach, so again, be open for feeling the one way if "better" than another.

Conventional

The conventional medical approach with which you are familiar focuses on the current problem. In veterinary school we are taught to use the symptoms an animal has now to find the physiological problem within the body and then use techniques or substances to eliminate the symptoms or "fix" the organ that has a problem. A dog with thin hair, lethargy and obesity may be diagnosed with hypothyroidism and given thyroid pills. This may eliminate current symptoms—until the next disease appears. An itching cat may be given steroid injections to stop the itch for now. Conventional drugs usually address the reactions of the body. Anti-inflammatory drugs effectively stop pain, redness, swelling, itching and heat in different parts of the body. Anti-emetics and anti-spasmodics stop vomiting and diarrhea. Anti-histamines decrease itching and redness. Sometimes conventional drugs replace a substance not being produced adequately in the body—insulin, thyroid hormone, ACTH. Often an animal will be given several medications at the same office visit—anti-inflammatory and anti-biotic ointment for the ears, anti-biotic and anti-spasmodic for the diarrhea and anti-histamines for the itching. The drugs are very effective and usually produce quick results. Many animals seem to do well on this approach and their problems quickly resolve. Others act older or more ill even if their current problems resolve. Now you will be able to tell if your animal is really responding in a curative way to the current treatment. As mentioned on page 9, when an animal is responding curatively, the current symptoms all slowly resolve and the animal feels healthier and happier in all ways. If the symptoms resolve but your animal is less active, stiffer, pickier about foods previously loved or has negative behavior changes, the treatment has not been good for your animal and you need to try a different approach—acupuncture, homeopathy, herbs or other holistic modality.

Something different—Holistic

"Holistic" is an approach to thinking about health that focuses on the whole animal rather than a "disease." The holistic approach uses both conventional and alternative treatments. Holistic practitioners are taught to use all the symptoms an animal has now and has ever had in the past to find and treat the individual's underlying predisposition to illness. Each dog with thin hair, lethargy and obesity may need a different homeopathic remedy or different acupuncture point prescription. Each itching cat may regain his or her health with one of the different treatment options available. When treatments are successful, the current symptoms resolve over time, never come back, the animal is more active, feels better and no further treatment is needed. This journal is the cornerstone of the holistic approach because it helps you evaluate your animal's total health and response to treatment.

A palette of choices

Think of an artist's palette with many different colors of paint as this holistic approach. The palette is the approach of focusing on the whole animal and paying attention to the response to each treatment. Each different color of paint is a type of treatment—conventional drugs, conventional surgery, conventional lab work, classical homeopathy, combination homeopathy, needle acupuncture, laser acupuncture, traditional Chinese medicine, chiropractic, network chiropractic, herbs, flower essences, massage and more. Your animal's life is the painting. Some paintings need only one color and others need many different colors to be beautiful. Conventional treatments, or homeopathy, or herbs or another may be the only approach needed to maintain health, or many different treatment approaches may be essential.

The underlying philosophy of holistic medicine

Shifting how you view symptoms and illness is a key step to having your animal be very healthy. The premise (the palette) is to treat the individual who has the disease, not merely the disease. Since the underlying energy imbalance is being addressed, treatments will address all the current symptoms at the same time. The itching, ear and digestive problems will be given a single energetic treatment. General health building supplements, mild topical treatments to soothe the skin and ears and gentle energy techniques may be also used. The main treatment is to re-balance the energetic basis of the body so the symptoms never return and there is general improvement in health. Physicists have now validated this energy approach, so read some of their material. Just as no two snowflakes are the same, no two animals have identical underlying problems. The treatment is chosen for each animal, not for the disease. If you glance quickly at snowflakes they may appear the same, yet they are unique. The same symptoms in different animals seem to need the same treatment, yet to achieve true health each animal may need a different combination of modalities, different homeopathic remedies, chiropractic or acupuncture prescriptions.

Pasteur said *"the microbe is nothing, the terrain everything."* Terrain refers to the individual's specific susceptibility to disease, including infectious agents. Where did the susceptibility come from? Can it be eliminated? Every generation and culture that looks at this deep level of "spirit" has different explanations for the cause of ill health. As you explore different way of healing your animals you will be sharing a journey followed by billions of people through the centuries. Try something yourself or with professional help, then evaluate its effect on your animal by carefully keeping the journal.

The path of health

We all desire symptoms to disappear quickly so our animals feel better. How we get rid of the symptoms can influence future health. The most deeply healing approach is to have the internal energy field (vital force) become balanced (not ill) which will then stop the compensatory symptoms from occurring. The body produces symptoms to heal the deep energy imbalance. Artificially suppressing symptoms with treatments (alternative or conventional) merely puts a temporary stop to the problem or even furthers weakens the energy field leading to more serious problems in the future and often a shorter lifespan.

When a successful treatment is given there is often an initial primary effect that is due to both the individual's energy field and the treatment itself. This is followed by a critical secondary effect generated by the energy field regaining health, causing it to "clean house." The "dust" (current symptoms) is gone along with the tendency to allow the "dust" to accumulate again. Stressors (vaccines, diet, emotions, environment, drugs, etc.) can again imbalance the energy field so it produces symptoms and needs more treatment.

Health is not a place we get to—it is a journey. Each animal has a different path. It is up to us to observe carefully, keep a journal, treat carefully and wait long enough for the inner energetic field to demonstrate in which direction the healing is progressing. No one veterinarian, no one book, no one expert, no one approach can be predicted as the best for your animal. Since you live with your animals and observe them carefully and have chosen specific life styles (diet, exercise, vaccination, etc) you must insist that practitioners at least honor the choices you have made for health for your animals. They may certainly disagree and try to convince you of their opinion. Use the knowledge you have learned about the anatomy and physiology of animals, the principles behind different treatments, read a lot, call someone, attend one of the Healthy Animals Teleclasses to keep your animal moving towards better and better health.

CASE HISTORIES—DIFFERENT CHOICES ON THE PATH TO HEALTH

Midnight was diagnosed with low thyroid at age 2 and put on Soloxine. Her hair grew back in and she lost weight, but the owners felt she had "matured" and did not play as much. Two years later she developed a vaginal infection after her annual vaccination that was treated with antibiotics. Then she was very lethargic for 5-6 months and then her energy returned with no additional treatments. The next two years followed the same pattern, with increasing months of lethargy. The drugs have eliminated the current symptoms yet she feels more ill overall (suppression). These had not been good choices for Midnight, so her owner looked for a different approach so she would not be tired most of the year. When all the symptoms and reaction to drugs and vaccines were incorporated into the treatment selection of homeopathic remedies and other lifestyle changes including a raw meat and fresh food diet, Midnight bounced with energy, great hair coat and had a normal weight for many more years (a cure).

Sue, the Siamese, lived to 22. She did not seem to grow old until she was 18. She had several skin problems that were treated with antibiotics and antihistamines. When she was 14 she developed a hyperactive thyroid and had surgery. She recovered rapidly and continued to be active for a few more years. The drugs, canned food and vaccines were appropriate choices for this cat.

Rosie, a Great Dane who had other problems during her life, developed a spinal compression as the result of a fall that pinched her spinal cord. Her rear became progressively weaker. Her owners had been using homeopathy, good nutrition, massage and did not vaccinate. She continued to deteriorate until she could often not get up by herself. The owners tried acupuncture twice a week. After 4 months of treatment, she began to improve steadily and after a year was walking 60% of normal and showed no further improvement. She was walking, getting up by herself and hopping into the back of the truck when it was backed up to the curb, giving her about a foot or a little more to negotiate. Trying a different approach, the owners started giving the dogs the N'Zymes products and saw further improvement from there. She is actually trotting now, though for no more than a dozen strides. She and her owners are very proud. She is gaining in muscle. She is still having acupuncture once a week. Her owners will continue to keep track of all of her symptoms in a journal and will try other approaches on Rosie's journey to health.

DEFINITIONS OF ALTERNATIVE TREATMENT TECHNIQUES

The following definitions are very brief and express my personal experience. There are many more. The first are healing techniques you can and should learn yourself. They will often soothe the symptoms while deep healing is occurring. To find training in the following techniques first go to your local health food store, holistic health practitioner or search on the web. Many are used primarily to treat people. Learn it as taught to treat humans, then apply to animals. Some are specifically for animals. Both approaches are the same, since we are all energy beings. The second group requires training, certification or licensing. Some of these have certification programs with a year or more of courses, exams and evaluation of clinical ability.

Techniques You Can Learn Yourself

Tellington TTouch: Every owner and person working with animals will love this easy to learn healing technique. TTouch is a method based on making gently circular movements of the fingers and hands all over the body, including the face and even the gums. The intent of TTouch is to activate the function of the cells and awaken cellular intelligence. TTouch can help animals learn better, relax, pay attention and can heal many ailments. www. Tteam-ttouch.com.

Reiki: The practitioner places her hands upon the animal (or it can be done from a distance as some animals are too sensitive for direct touch) with the intent for healing to occur. The energy flows through the healer into the animal. This is based on directly applying Chi (energy) to rebalance the energy field so it no longer needs to produce the physical symptoms. It is a very good adjunct to any healing modality, especially to relieve pain and inflammation. www.reiki.org is one site.

Flower Essences: Totally safe liquids extracted from flowers, these are wonderful support for healing of animals and people. They are especially good in emotional problems. Green Hope Farms and Anaflora have combination flower essences that are very effective in preventing fleas and ticks on your animals. The "emergency" essences are great to have on hand. Remember that you may need to take the same essences as your animals. www.LittleBigCat.com, www.greenhopeessences.com, www.anaflora.com.

Massage: This is always nice for all beings. It stimulates the body to heal by relaxing muscles holding the bones, joints and organs in improper position and everyone can do it. Michael Fox's *Healing Touch* (His other books, some now out of print are excellent and will soon be available on his web site —*Touchlings and One Mind, One Earth*) is one good resource.

Aroma Therapy: Aromatherapy uses aromatic, volatile extracts of plants to treat emotional problems in animals and people. By correcting the emotional imbalance, physical problems can be eased as well. Basil, Geranium and Lavender, among others, have a calming effect. Lemon has a cleansing effect. Use caution with cats as some essential oils can be toxic. Their smell is so acute that they may be bothered by the oils difused in a room they cannot leave. How can you tell? You are right—read your journal critically. www.PulseParty.com/132195, Aromaleigh.com and www.thePetWhisperer.com are good sources.

Magnets: Medical benefits work via bio-electrical (electro-biochemical) effects at the cellular level. The electro-motive force exerted by the magnetic field will re-organize molecules within the cell and thus affect biochemical processes. Magnets have been particularly effective in pain management from arthritis or old age. They have been effective in many other illnesses as well. Nikkan is a great source of good magnets.

Pressure point therapy: Chinese medicine is based on the principles of energy flow throughout the body on meridians. There are specific points that access these meridians. Anyone can learn how to press on these acupressure points to relieve symptoms or assist with healing. *Four Paws, Five Directions* by Cheryl Schwartz is a wonderful guide to this therapy. Learn from your acupuncture veterinarian specific points to help your animal's problem.

 **Herbal:** Use of the medicinal herbs in their material form to treat specific problems, conditions or to enhance overall vitality. Mild ones like slippery elm, burdock, dandelion, comfrey, dill, Echinacea, eyebright, garlic, ginseng, goldenseal, horsetail, kombu, myrrh, nettle, parsley, plantain, psyllium seeds, and others are fairly safe for you to try on your own. Remember that some plants can be toxic. Books by Tilford, DeBaircle Levy, Wood, Yarnall, Frazier & Pitcairn cover herbal treatment of animals. One of the problems is administration—especially in cats. Animals' Apawthecary has glycerin extracts that are very good for cats and dogs since they are more palatable. Herbs can be toxic. (www.ChristinaChambreau.com)

Nutraceuticals and food supplements: Nutritional substances are used to enhance the body's function. Again, the problem is often how to administer these to cats or small dogs. Large dogs take the capsules, tablets and powders with no problem and some are made in a tasty base.

Healing/Animal Communicators: A leap in faith for some, these modalities can produce miracles. The next 50 years will find many more people being healed by directed energy methods that intuitive healers can use. Each communicator receives "messages" from your animal friend in a different way, always requiring their interpretation. As with all methods of treatment or input, you need to notice if what they say fits and improves your animal's life by keeping up with journal entries, especially for a short time before and after the consut..

Color Therapy: Color is visible light emitted or reflected at a specific vibrational wavelength; it is this unique vibrational signature which produces the healing effect. The blue colors are calming and the red, of course, are stimulating.

Crystals: Crystals produce a small electrical charge when pressed or put in water. They can give energy to the cells for self repair. Quartz crystals are the most common and come in different shapes and colors for different effects and to stimulate different chakras. Animals often will select their own crystal.

Prayer: Scientific studies have proven the efficacy of prayer.

Professional Training Is Needed For These Approaches

Homeopathy: System of medicine started in 1800 that uses substances (in their energetic form) to correct deficits in the vital force so symptoms resolve and overall health is enhanced. Remedies that produce symptoms in tests (provings) are given to ill animals (or people) who have the same pattern of symptoms. Certification.

Chinese Medicine (Acupuncture & Chinese Herbs): 5,000 year old system that treats the energy pathways of the body to remove blockages and rebalance the chi. Needles, moxabustion, lasers, single and combination Chinese herbs are some of the treatments used in Chinese medicine. Certification.

Chiropractic: Re-aligning the musculoskeletal system, especially the spinal column, relieves pressure on nerves, thus restoring function to the body. Certification.

Network Chiropractic: A more gentle modification of chiropractic using light pressure and energy techniques for a more gentle chiropractic treatment. Training.

Ayurveda: A system of medicine from India using herbs to balance the prana. Training for treating people adapts well to animals.

Bowen: Physical manipulation of the muscles based on "strumming" the muscle body to readjust the way it moves and connects with the body. Bowen trained veterinarians are few at this time and are reporting deep healing from this technique.

CASE HISTORIES OF ANIMALS ON
THE PATH TO HEALTH

Isis, an Egyptian Mau cat, came to her owner a bit young, at 6 weeks of age and already had a slight cough. Conventional drugs did not seem to help over the next 4 years, but the cough never was very severe, just persistent. Isis also was not very playful and though nice, never sat in Phil's lap. When she got her 6 vaccines at age 5, she had a severe asthmatic coughing reaction, was rushed to the hospital for oxygen and treatment. For the next year and half she had to be on 4 drugs to stay alive. She still had breathing trouble and sometimes had to go to the hospital for oxygen therapy. Within 2 months of beginning homeopathic treatment she was off all medications including homeopathic ones, affectionate, lap sitting, purring, active, playful and had no asthma attacks. 8 years later she had to go to a new home and is still healthy.

Molly was very ill when adopted at 10 weeks with sneezing, coughing, small, crooked bones and big staring eyes. With a fresh food diet, herbs, massage and homeopathy, she became completely healthy except for a sinus inflammation that caused her to often breathe with a very noisy in and out breath. Homeopathic remedies made no difference over the next 4 months, though she contin-  ued to be healthy in every other way. An intuitive healer worked for 3 weeks and she has been symptom free for 6 months. Reiki and T-Touch help when she is nervous and flower essences have lowered the number of fleas and ticks.

 **Pitzie** had vomited constantly. A biopsy diag- nosed inflammatory bowel disease. She did not want to touched at all and would lick hysterical- ly and run away. She was on a mixture of drugs. When young she had a mast cell tumor removed from her abdomen. At 10 years of age she acted like a kitten, still had skin and vomiting problems, was on the drugs and developed a tiny mass on her ear that one veterinarian felt was a tumor and recommended surgery to remove the entire ear. This time the owner did not want to do surgery as she was trying to heal the aversion to touch, vomiting, licking herself and other things like the walls. Six months of homeopathic treatment and the ear lumps (more had appeared) had completely disappeared, she was super active and playful, 50% better about being touched and handled although she was still vomiting and not yet cured.

CHOOSING A VETERINARIAN AND HAVING THE BEST HEALING PARTNERSHIP

The Humane Society of the United States gives great advice on their web site about selecting a veterinarian. Go to their site, www.hsus.org to read the entire article, which includes *"You're looking for someone to meet your needs and those of your pet, a doctor who has people as well as animal skills...You will likely want to evaluate the entire veterinary team's competence and caring...You will probably be happier if you drive a few extra miles or pay a few extra dollars to get the care you desire for your pet. Ask people who have the same approach to pet care as you. Once you've narrowed your search, schedule a visit to meet the staff, tour the facility, and learn about the hospital's philosophy and policies."*

The American Veterinary Medical Association says much the same on their web site, www.avma.org. *"In selecting a veterinarian, your goals should be to find the doctor that best meets your needs and to establish a long-term relationship. The veterinarian will maintain a history of your pet, including health records that detail immunizations, reactions to medications, behavior traits, etc. So, it's important to see your veterinarian for all your pet's health care needs. Your veterinarian will know the best preventive and critical care to provide with your pet's individual health care needs in mind. All veterinarians are special. All pets are special. Take the time to choose the right veterinarian for your special pet."*

Both sites emphasize the need to start now to find the best veterinarian. I highly encourage you to explore the variety of veterinary care available in your area now. Do not wait until there is a crisis and you need care immediately. There are veterinarians who make house calls, have a one person practice, have large staffs and lots of state-of-the-art equipment, offer some holistic care, offer only holistic, offer only one type of medicine or see only one type of animal. First decide what type of medicine you wish for your animal at this time. Then research the different possibilities. There are many guidelines on the web in addition to the two I quoted above. Put "selecting a veterinarian" into a search engine. Also, many veterinarians now have web sites, so read several to get ideas of the services you would like to see in your ideal practice. Ask your local clinics if they offer these services. If stumped, call 1-866-4-VET NOW.

Finding Holistic Veterinary care

While there are many conventional veterinarians from whom to choose in your local area, fewer are holistically trained. The above guidelines apply and then you should look for some specific qualities. Holistic medicine takes the perspective of treating the whole animal. Even if there is a current problem, for example diarrhea or itching, a good holistic veterinarian will ask questions about what problems there have been in the past, what changes in the household or the environment may have triggered the current complaint and if there is anything that makes the current complaints better or worse. They will also evaluate the overall energy level of the animal at every visit. Their goal is to make the animal healthier for life, not just to get rid of the current symptom. They will educate you and explain what they see when physically examining your animal. They will give you a range of treatment options and listen to your suggestions. Most are very willing for you to try another type of veterinary care and return to them when you wish.

Modalities used by holistic veterinarians usually include ones listed previously (see page 45). Some individuals will be wonderful with your animal—others will be great at explaining to you what is happening with your animals. A few are good in both areas. Few veterinarians are perfect, and we all have bad days. Your animal should at least be comfortable with your choice, you should be able to get your questions and concerns addressed and the health of your animal (according to your journal keeping) should be moving in a positive direction in all ways.

Creating a healing team

One veterinarian may fulfill what your animal needs to become and stay healthy. Or you may need a team of several veterinarians and energy healers as becoming trained yourself in some healing techniques. The number of veterinarians trained in alternative methods is rapidly increasing, so the first place to look is in your own city. Call the local health food store or holistic health practitioner (chiropractor, acupuncturist, etc.) and ask if they know of any holistic veterinarians who are open to supporting your holistic work with your animals. The Veterinary Advice Line connects you directly with a holistic veterinarian who will discuss your animal's problem for $34.99. They will help you decide on the next course of action and refer you to someone in your area or a veterinarian with whom you can consult by telephone. Call 1-866-4-VET NOW or go to their web site, www.vetadviceline.com.

The Internet is your next tool since most organizations have web sites and many breed associations and concerned pet owners have web sites that share names of good holistic veterinarians. Many veterinary organizations also have phone numbers that you can use, but since offices may not be well staffed it will be quicker to use the Internet. The information below should help you find the most appropriate holistic veterinarian for your pet. Please note that the lists of veterinarians on these web sites may not always be up-to-date. If your first attempts lead nowhere, don't give up, keep trying!

Academy of Veterinary Homeopathy
P.O. Box 9280
Wilmington, DE 19809
Phone: 866-652-1590
E-mail: webmaster@acadvethom.org
Website: www.theAVH.org
• Good list of members, many of whom work by phone.

American Academy of Veterinary Acupuncture
PO Box 419
Hygiene, CO 80533-0419
Phone: 303-772-6726
E-mail: AAVAoffice@aol.com
Website: www.aava.org

American Holistic Veterinary Medical Association
2218 Old Emmorton Road
Bel Air, MD 21014
Phone: 410-569-0795
Fax: 410-569-2346
E-mail: AHVMA@compuserve.com
Website: www.ahvma.org
• Lists all the members by state. (Not always current)

Veterinary Chiropractic Association
623 Main Street
Hillsdale, IL 61257
Phone: 309-658-2920
Fax: 309-658-2622
E-mail: AmVetChiro@aol.com
Website: www.animalchiropractic.org

International Veterinary Acupuncture Society
PO Box 271395
Fort Collins, CO 80527
Phone: 970-266-0666
Fax: 970-266-0777
E-mail: IVASOffice@aol.com
Website: www.ivas.org

Assessing a potential veterinarian's skills and working with them

Once you have several recommendations, how do you select one to start with and then how do you know if you are getting good service? First view their web site if they have one. You will learn the training, credentials, practice philosophy and a bit about the veterinarian's style.

Ask the veterinarian in whom you are interested:

1. What modalities are used? (Acupuncture, Homeopathy, Chinese herbs, Western herbs...)

2. What is their training?

3. Is their goal overall health or to merely treat the current complaint?

4. To what organizations do they belong?

As she treats your animal, a good holistic veterinarian will usually:

1. Ask about the history, overall energy, diet, what might have caused the current problem, the environment and what makes the symptoms better or worse.

2. Their physical exam will be gentle, complete and they will show you (you may need to ask) what they mean by "gingivitis, big lymph nodes, heart murmur", etc.

3. They will be willing to answer your questions and explain why they are recommending a particular treatment.

4. If they recommend conventional treatments (antibiotics, prednisone, etc.) they will explain to you why they are choosing this over holistic, and give you a chance to request the more holistic treatment.

5. They will not do anything (vaccinate, treat) without asking you first.

6. They will recommend fewer or no vaccinations and a raw meat or at least more holistic diet.

7. They will schedule follow up appointments until your animal is really healthy. You will know your animal is feeling better overall and has few to none of the symptoms of underlying illness. (see page 5)

What you can do to help your holistic veterinarian:

1. Keep a dated journal of any problems, even little ones.

2. Write down any treatments given.

3. Call if symptoms worsen, or they are less energetic and less happy, or you have concerns.

How will keeping a journal help your animal be healthier and you happier?

Keeping a journal is one of the most important steps you can take to have your animals live their longest, be the healthiest and even to produce the healthiest offspring. You and your veterinarian (especially the holistic ones) will be able to help your animal more effectively when you can give all this information

Having recorded wonderful memories of your animal and the way she has improved with the different treatments you discovered will certainly help you be happier. Some people do small sketches as well, or paste in pictures of their animal.

There are infinite number of ways to keep this journal—be creative.

ABOUT THE AUTHOR

Christina Chambreau, DVM, is an internationally known homeopathic veterinarian and lecturer. She was a veterinary technician from the age of 10 and became active in The Hunger Project in 1978. Graduating from the University of Georgia Veterinary College in 1980, she began using homeopathy in her veterinary practice in 1983, and has used primarily homeopathy since 1988. A dynamic teacher, Dr. Chambreau began teaching the Ending Hunger Briefings and trained many speakers. She is a founder of the Academy Of Veterinary Homeopathy and is on the faculty of the National Center for Homeopathy Summer School. As vice president in charge of the Veterinary Advice Line, she provides a referral service so people can find the best care for their animal's specific problem. She lectures about 20 times per year, including for the Atlantic Coast Veterinary Conference, North American Veterinary Conference, Midwest Veterinary Conference, Virginia Veterinary Conference, Virginia and D.C. Academy Veterinary Technician meetings, Groom Expo, American Boarding Kennel Association, breed shows, health food stores, and more. She has written and is quoted in many magazines & books. She is co-author of the *Homeopathic Repertory: A Tutorial* and *How To Have A Stress Free Wedding*. She is frequently on radio (go to caringforcreatures.com/onairf.html to hear her) and TV shows and teaches 1-10 day courses on health for animals. She is married to Dr. Mort Orman, author of the *14-day Stress Cure* and *How To Have A Stress Free Wedding*. Her 16 year old daughter is a drummer and committed to building a free college and orphanage in Africa.

Catalina Smith is President and Founder of *Corporate Creative Associates* a marketing communications firm based in New York and Washington, D.C. She is an Emmy award winning director and producer. She has a broad range of healthcare, (both allopathic and alternative) pharmaceutical and information technology experience. She is on the Executive Board of the American Society of Consultant Pharmacists Foundation. A Phi Beta Kappa and Fulbright scholar, Catalina teaches media production at several universities. "Cat" is an avid theatre director and actress, speaks fluent Spanish and continues to be enchanted by and grateful for her three cats and husband Giuseppe.

C. Liane Luini is CEO of *Luini Unlimited*, a desktop publishing, web design company in Landover Hills, Maryland. She is also a dog obedience trainer who teaches group and private classes using operant conditioning. She trains and shows her own dogs in obedience competition. Her adoption of the Misters Toby and Flaki, brought her to both training and holistic treatment of animals culminating in the opportunity to collaborate on this Journal. She will be eternally grateful to both boys for the journey they started and have shared with her.

BRIGHTHAVEN

There are many wonderful rescue groups and shelters in the world. Each one has a unique approach, works with different animals and is saving lives. My favorite is BrightHaven. Gail and Richard Pope began BrightHaven 12 years ago when Gail realized she wanted to give a home to old cats for the rest of their lives. I taught a course on holistic health and homeopathy organized by one of their animal communicators. Gail then began to shift to using holistic methods in her home. BrightHaven is now a retirement retreat for over 90 senior and disabled animals. They are dedicated to the rescue, care and enhancement of the lives of these special animals. Most cats are 16 or older when they enter.

One cat I treated lived to 27, and many make it to 20-25. They are dedicated to a program of research and education, arising from the miraculous results they have seen when the balance of natural feeding, holistic care and modern medicine are used in a loving family environment. Visiting BrightHaven is awesome and I am so touched by their caring home. Gail, her mom and staff have a way of interacting with the soul of the animal, not the ill body. They treat cats as if they will live forever, knowing that they may die tomorrow. One veterinarian who visited BrightHaven described her "escort" cat. This emaciated, wobbly old cat was at the door as I entered. He greeted me and followed or led me from room to room. Even though weak and clearly very old, he had a job and loved doing it. Please visit www.BrightHaven.org or visit them in Northern California. Help by contributing financially, donating therapeutic healing, visiting and cleaning.

THE HUNGER PROJECT

Why am I talking about ending hunger for people in a book about having your animals become super healthy? I believe that The Hunger Project has the solution for all the hunger, wars, poverty, abuse of women and environmental problems of the world. If we can create a world that, like Bucky Fuller said, "Works for everyone", our companion animals as well as wild ones will have a safer life with more chances of living long and healthy lives. Imagine, for a minute, a world where every person has a fabulous vision, knows they are the one to make their vision become reality and are taking action steps now. The Hunger Project has local people lead Vision, Commitment and Action workshops around the world. They have developed an empowerment program that follows these workshops with national political support, media coverage and continuing support. They always ask the question, "What more needs to be done to eliminate hunger and poverty in this area?" and then act on the answer with powerful, innovative programs. Because we believe that empowering, not helping, is the answer, your contribution is not to go to India to work. You and I can allocate our personal resources (money) to impact on the health of the planet as well as provide comfortably for ourselves. I contribute on a regular basis to many organizations and think The Hunger Project gives the most long term benefit for my investment. Go to www.THP.org for wonderful, uplifting, positive information about the transformations happening around the world. This is a great antidote to most media coverage of the world. Put "Orman" in the search box to see my daughter and myself on an investor's trip to Senegal several years ago. Read the section of why it is important to invest in The Hunger Project and re-allocate as much money as you can to invest in The Hunger Project.

_____'s Biography Page

_____'s Timeline of Health and Major Events

_____

_____

_____

_____

_____

_____

_____

_____

_____

_____

_____

_____

_____

_____

_____

_____

There must be a beginning of any great matter, but the continuing unto the end until it be thoroughly finished yield the true glory.

—Sir Francis Drake

Healthy Animal's Journal

We give dogs time we can spare, space we can spare and love we can spare. In return, dogs give us their all. It's the best deal man has ever made.

—M. Facklam

Healthy Animal's Journal

_____

_____

_____

_____

_____

_____

_____

_____

_____

_____

_____

_____

_____

_____

_____

_____

_____

_____

_____

_____

_____

_____

_____

_____

_____

_____

_____

_____

_____

_____

_____

_____

_____

_____

_____

_The reason a dog has so many friends
is that he wags his tail instead of his
tongue._
—Anonymous

Healthy Animal's Journal

_____

_____

_____

_____

_____

_____

_____

_____

_____

_____

_____

_____

_____

_____

_____

_____

If your dog is fat, you aren't getting enough exercise.
—Unknown

_____

_____

_____

_____

_____

_____

_____

_____

_____

_____

_____

_____

_____

_____

_____

_____

_____

_____

*There is no psychiatrist in the world
like a puppy licking your face.*
—Ben Williams

A dog is the only thing on earth that loves you more than he loves himself.
—Josh Billings

Healthy Animal's Journal

_____

_____

_____

_____

_____

_____

_____

_____

_____

_____

_____

_____

_____

_____

Healthy Animal's Journal

_____

_____

_____

_____

_____

_____

*The average dog is a nicer person
than the average person.*
—Andy Rooney
_____

_____

_____

_____

_____

_____

_____

_____

_____

_____

_____

Outside of a dog, a book is probably man's best friend; inside of a dog, it's too dark to read.
—Groucho Marx

Ever consider what they must think of us? I mean, here we come back from a grocery store with the most amazing haul—chicken, pork, half a cow. They must think we're the greatest hunters on earth!

—Anne Tyler

If I have any beliefs about immortality, it is that certain dogs I have known will go to heaven, and very, very few persons.

—James Thurber

Healthy Animal's Journal

_____

_____

_____

_____

_____

_____

_____

_____

_____

_____

_____

_____

_____

_____

_____

_____

_____

_____

Healthy Animal's Journal

Women and cats will do as they please, and men and dogs should relax and get used to the idea.
—Robert A. Heinlein

Healthy Animal's Journal

It is hard to fail, but it is worse never to have tried to succeed. In this life we get nothing save by effort.
—Teddy Roosevelt

Healthy Animal's Journal

The supreme happiness in life is knowing that we are loved.
—Victor Hugo

_____

_____

_____

_____

_____

_____

_____

_____

_____

_____

_____

_____

_____

_____

_____

_____

_____

Act quickly. Think slowly.
—Greek proverb

You are thinking slowly by using your animal's symptoms to evaluate their health progress. Then you can take quick action when needed.

_____

_____

_____

_____

_____

_____

_____

_____

_____

_____

_____

_____

_____

_____

Some animals make the world more special just by being in it.

Healthy Animal's Journal

Healthy Animal's Journal

> *The more I learn about homeopathy, the more I realize how personal and individual it is.*
> —Madelyn Reilly

_____

_____

_____

_____

_____

_____

_____

_____

_____

_____

_____

_____

_____

_____

_____

_____

Your heart speaks, take good notes.
—Yurok Indians

Healthy Animal's Journal

Make large wishes, focus on them, and watch them materialize. I wish for health and love for all animals.

Homeopathy made a magic contribution to my life and my canines and felines.
—Susan Kasper

_____

_____

_____

_____

_____

_____

_____

_____

_____

_____

_____

_____

_____

_____

Whenever I remember you my heart is happy.
—Sioux Indians

Healthy Animal's Journal

Your animal believes in you and trusts you totally.

A hug is a perfect gift.

What a blessed and rich life this is. May we serve to magnify the joy of each other always.
—Dr. Lori Tapp

_____'s Treatment Summary Page